water
paintings

Books in the Linkers series

First published 1996 A&C Black (Publishers) Limited
35 Bedford Row, London WC1R 4JH

ISBN 0-7136-4370-6
A CIP catalogue record for this book is available from the British Library.

Copyright © 1996 BryantMole Books

Commissioned photographs by Zul Mukhida
Design by Jean Wheeler   Picture research by Liz Harman

Consultants: Grant Jones, Art Adviser, E. Sussex
Ian Punter, Adviser in Design Technology, E. Sussex

The publishers would like to thank the children of Northiam C.E. School, East Sussex, who worked so hard to produce the artwork featured in this book, and Judy Grahame who facilitated and guided its production.

Acknowledgements

Bridgeman Art Library; Pushkin Museum, Moscow 21 (top), Guildhall Art Gallery, Corporation of London 21 (bottom), Chapel Studios; Tim Richardson 8 (left), Jayne Knights 12 (left), Edward Parker; 6 (left), Eye Ubiquitious; E. Boyes Amers 8 (right), Positive Images; 3 (right), 4 (right), 10 (left), 16 (top), Tony Stone Images; Arnulf Husmo 3 (left), Visual Arts Library; Paris, Louvre 14 (top), National Gallery, London 20.

Printed and bound in Italy by L.E.G.O.

Water

discovered through
Art and Technology

Karen Bryant-Mole

Contents

A & C Black • London

Water

Water plays a very important part in our everyday lives.

We use water on the outside of our bodies when we wash.
We use water inside our bodies when we drink.

We see water all
around us, in seas,
in rivers and
in lakes.

There is water in our
weather, too.
It makes everything wet
on a rainy day.

In this book, you will find
ideas that help you to
explore water through art,
design and technology.

Waterproof clothes

This boy is wearing a rain cape.
Clothes that are designed to be worn in
the rain have to be waterproof.

Why not make your own waterproof
coat or cape?

You will need to use a waterproof material,
such as plastic. You could use the plastic from
a carrier bag or bin bag.

The materials you use to join the pieces together
will need to be waterproof, too.

You might find it helpful to make a watertight
joint, or seam, when you join up two pieces.
You could do this by rolling the edges
of the pieces together.

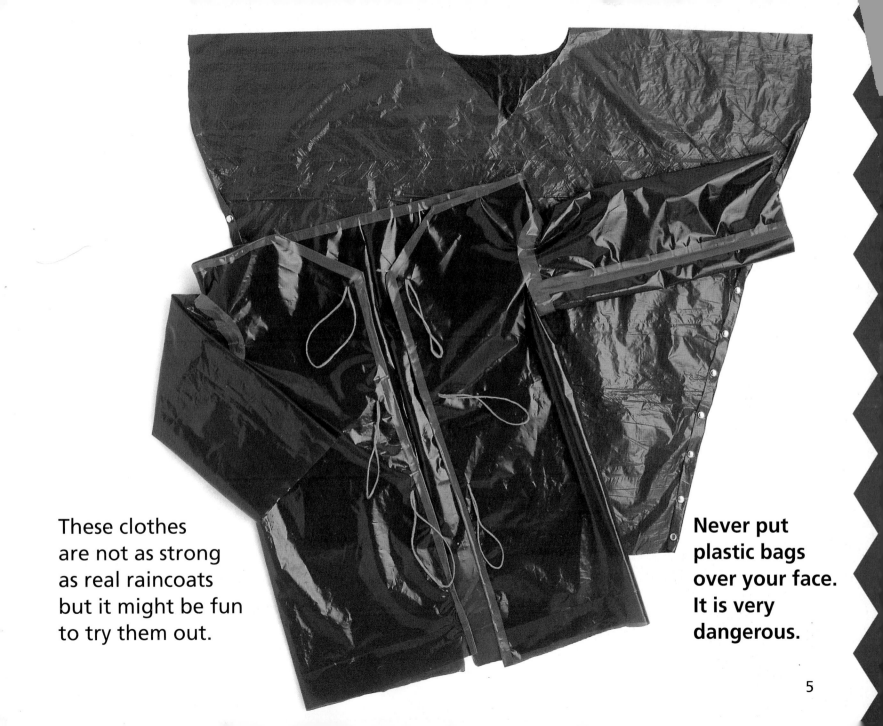

These clothes are not as strong as real raincoats but it might be fun to try them out.

Never put plastic bags over your face. It is very dangerous.

5

Waterproof patterns

When this duck gets out of the pond, the water will run off its feathers.

You will need something oily or waxy to draw with.
You could use oil pastels, wax crayons or even an old candle.

You will also need some very thin paint or drawing ink.

The water does so because the feathers are coated with a special oil. You can use this idea to make pictures and patterns.

Draw your pattern or picture.
When you brush the watery paint or ink over the
paper it will run off the places where you have
drawn but soak into the paper everywhere else.

Keeping clean

The car in this picture is going through a car wash.
The machine washes the car, while the driver sits inside.

Wouldn't it be fun if there was a machine that washed people? You could design your own 'person wash'.

Think of all the things that you would need your machine to do.

Here are some finished designs.
You could use some of these ideas
in your own design.

Water dyes

This child is wearing clothes made from colourful fabrics.
Dyes are used to colour fabric.
Some dyes are called cold water dyes.
They are made from coloured powder mixed with water.

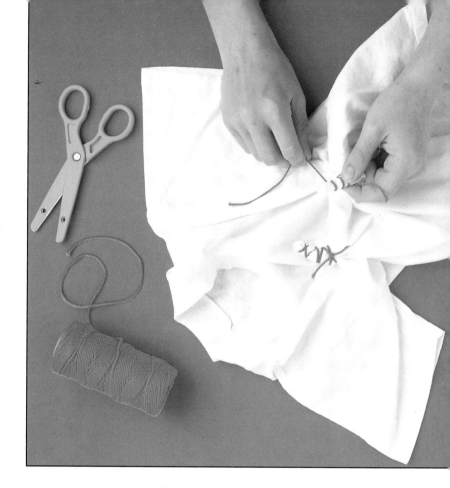

You can use old cotton T-shirts, string and cold water dyes to make your own, unique, clothes.
Bunch up a piece of T-shirt and wrap some string around it very tightly.
Do the same all over the T-shirt.

Ask an adult to dye the T-shirt for you,
following the instructions on the packet.
Do not try to dye it by yourself. Dyes stain.

When the T-shirt is dry,
remove the string.
You will see some
amazing patterns.

11

Rainwater gauge

Every day, information about our weather is collected.
This is a rainwater gauge.
It allows people to measure how much rain has fallen.

You will need to mark measurements on your gauge, so that you can compare the rainfall each day or week.
You can do this using a small container, such as an eggcup.
Mark the water-line each time you pour in an eggcupful of water.
The amount between each mark will be the same.

You could make your own rainwater gauge.

Here are some examples of rainwater gauges that children have made.

Don't forget, your gauge will have to be waterproof, too!

13

Watercolours

This picture is a watercolour.
Paints are made from coloured powders, called pigments, that have to be mixed with a liquid.
Watercolour paints are mixed with water.

Watercolour paints can be bought in tubes, in boxes, in pots or in bottles.
They can come as flat, hard 'cakes', thick liquids, powders, or even as crayons.

Children have used watercolour paints to make different designs.

The more water you use, the thinner and more watery the paint becomes.

The thicker the paint, the stronger the colour.

If you paint over a colour with another colour when the first colour is still wet, the colours will run into each other.

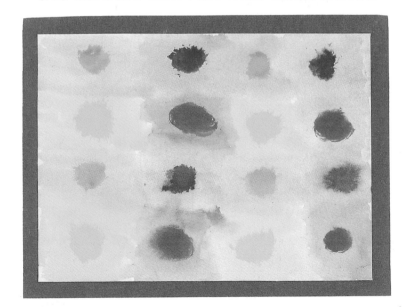

Floating

Some things float on water and some things sink.
The boat in this picture is floating on the sea.

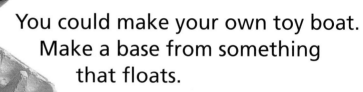

You could make your own toy boat.
Make a base from something that floats.
Test out a range of objects by putting them into a bowl of water.
The base should float evenly and not tip up.
It needs to be waterproof, too.
If not, it might break up or start to sink when the water soaks in.

When you add things to the base, you will have to keep checking that the boat has not become so heavy that it sinks.

You could play with your boat in the bath. How will you move it across the water?

Drying out

This box has been made from pâpier maché.

Pâpier maché is a mixture of paper, glue and water.

When the water in the mixture dries out, the pâpier maché becomes very hard and can then be painted.

To make something from pâpier maché, you will need some newspaper and some watery glue.

You could make a bowl by sticking strips of newspaper over part of a blown-up balloon.

Leave the pâpier maché to dry out.
When it is dry and hard,
pop the balloon.

Why not paint your pâpier maché bowl?

This bowl has been decorated to look
like a fish pond.

19

Water in art

Many artists have painted water in their pictures.
The paintings on these pages were all painted
just over a hundred years ago but each artist
has chosen a different style of painting.

This is a picture
by a French
painter called
Seurat.
The painting is
made up of
lots of tiny spots
of colour.

A Dutch painter
called van Gogh
painted this picture
by loading his
brush with oil
paint and making
bold brushstrokes
across the canvas.

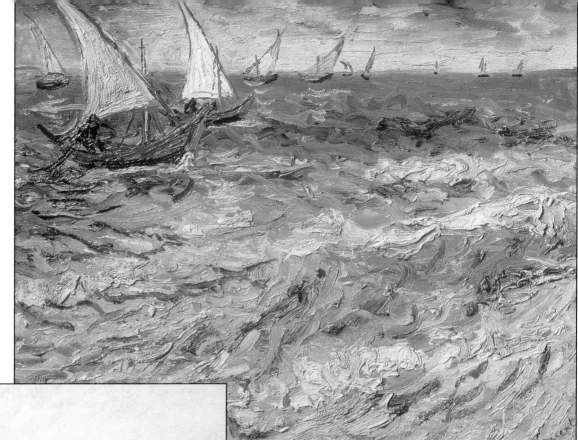

Here is a picture by an English
painter called Foster.
The watercolour paints that
he used give the river a watery,
flowing feel.

21

My water pictures

Here are some paintings of water that were made
by a group of children after they had looked at
other artists' work.

These paintings
have strong, thick
swirls of colour.

These watery pictures have been made using watercolour paints.

This effect was achieved using the side of a paintbrush.

Why don't you try experimenting with different ways of painting water?

23

Glossary

coated covered with a thin layer of something

designed made for a special purpose

fabric cloth

gauge an object that measures things

joint the place where two or more things meet

material what things are made from

pigment materials found in the ground, that can be used to colour paints

unique nothing else like it

Index

How to use this book

Each book in this series takes a familiar topic or theme and focuses on one area of the curriculum: science, art and technology, geography or history. The books are intended as starting points, illustrating some of the many different angles from which a topic can be studied. They should act as springboards for further investigation, activity or information seeking.

The following list of books may prove useful.

Further books to read

Series	Title	Author	Publisher
Creative Crafts	Fun with Paint	M. Butterfield	Heinemann
First Arts and Crafts	Painting	S. Stocks	Wayland
First Skills	Starting Painting	S. Mayes	Usborne
Get Set Go!	Painting Printing	R. Thompson	Watts
Jump! Starts Crafts	Pâpier Maché Play with Paint	James & Lynn	Watts
Looking at Art	Water in Art	R. Moore	Wayland
Making Pictures	Secrets of the Sea	King & Roundhall	Heinemann
Painting and Drawing	Watercolours	M. Comellia	A&C Black
Starting Technology	Water	J. Williams	Wayland
What Shall I Do Today?	What Shall I Paint?	R. Gibson	Usborne